CW01651229

CREEPY CRAWLIES

CREEPY CRAWLIES

POEMS BY
KATHY HARRISON

Front cover, frontispiece and 'Centipedes'
by Roz Wolseley-Charles.

GSP

Creepy Crawlies
Kathy Harrison

Published by Greyhound Self-Publishing 2012
Malvern, Worcestershire, United Kingdom.

Printed and bound by Aspect Design
89 Newtown Road, Malvern, Worcs. WR14 1PD
United Kingdom
Tel: 01684 561567
E-mail: books@aspect-design.net
Website: www.aspect-design.net

All Rights Reserved.

Copyright © 2012 Kathy Harrison

Kathy Harrison has asserted her moral right
to be identified as the author of this work.

The right of Kathy Harrison to be identified as the author
of this work has been asserted in accordance with
Section 77 of the Copyright, Designs and Patents Act 1988.

This book is sold subject to the condition that it shall not, by way of
trade or otherwise, be lent, resold, hired out or otherwise circulated
without the publisher's prior consent in any form of binding or cover
other than that in which it is published and without a similar condition
including this condition being imposed on the subsequent purchaser.

A copy of this book has been deposited with the British Library Board.

Cover Design Copyright © 2012 Aspect Design.
Original front cover, frontispiece and 'Centipedes' illustrations
by Roz Wolseley-Charles Copyright © 2012.

ISBN 978-1-909219-05-2

Contents

CREEPY CRAWLIES

There's a bug on my rug
A flea in my tea
A slug in the jug
And a bee after me.

There's a snail in the pail
A fly in the pie
There's ants in my pants
Butterflies in the sky.

There's a louse in the house,
A gnat in my hat
There's a moth in the broth –
And that, I hope, is that!

HARM NO LIVING THING

My mother's always telling me
To harm no living thing
Even nasty creepy crawlies
That bite and itch and sting.
I can't stamp on ants and spiders
Or swat the wasps and flies,
I can't collect the snails and slugs
'cause she warns me they will die.

My mum pretends she's never caused
Anything to die
She also makes out that she never
Ever tells a lie
But when she tidies round the house
I know that I have seen her
Sucking up the creepy crawlies
In her vacuum cleaner.
I said to her, how could she?
She said that they'd survive.
I think squashing them is kinder
Than burying them alive.

THE GOOD PLACE

I've got a really good place
To put my creepy crawlies
When I've dug around and got them
Out of the dirt
Worms and snails and earwigs
Slugs and spiders too
Where do I put them?
Down my sister's skirt.

FLEA

There's a flea in our carpet
That bites my ankles
Mum says it must come from the cat.
The cat wears a collar
To keep fleas away.
Mum hasn't an answer for that.

ANTS

Ants – an example to us all
Working together tirelessly,
Daring, tearing back and forth
To gather food from off the ground,
Caring, sharing with the others
Whatever tiny scraps they've found,
Searching for more, no time to rest,
Dragging food back to the nest.
Co-operation, never still,
Ceaseless activity, an ant hill.

CENTIPEDE

Tell me, little centipede,
How many legs you've got.
Some people say one hundred
But I think not.
When you walk by I try to see
How many I can spot,
But I only get as far as six
Then you've gone off like a shot.
I've given up now, centipede,
But I'll tell you what,
I'll settle for the answer
That it's really quite a lot.

MAGGOTS

Maggots
Wriggling, wiggling,
Twisting, turning,
Burrowing, feeding,
Growing fatter.

Maggots everywhere.
What's the matter?
Maggots – YUK!

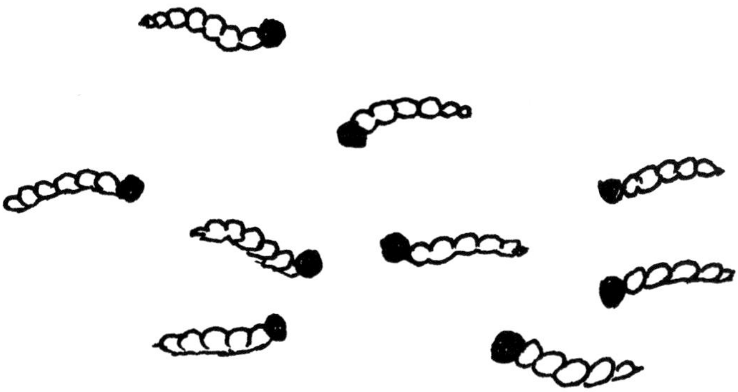

WOODLOUSE

My sister flicked a woodlouse
Across the kitchen floor
It rolled just like a football
It rolled right out the door.

I went outside to find it
To check it was OK
I found it by the garden wall
A ball all hard and grey.

The tiny ball uncurled then
As I watched it lying there
Opening itself the wrong way up
Legs flapping in the air.

It tried to turn back over
And I watched it as it tried
Then I gently flipped it on its front
And it ran away to hide.

THE HAIRY CATERPILLAR

I had a hairy caterpillar,
I kept it in a pot,
I gave it green leaves every day,
It really ate a lot.

It was growing bigger all the time,
It was getting rather fat.
Then it escaped off down the road
And ended up completely flat.

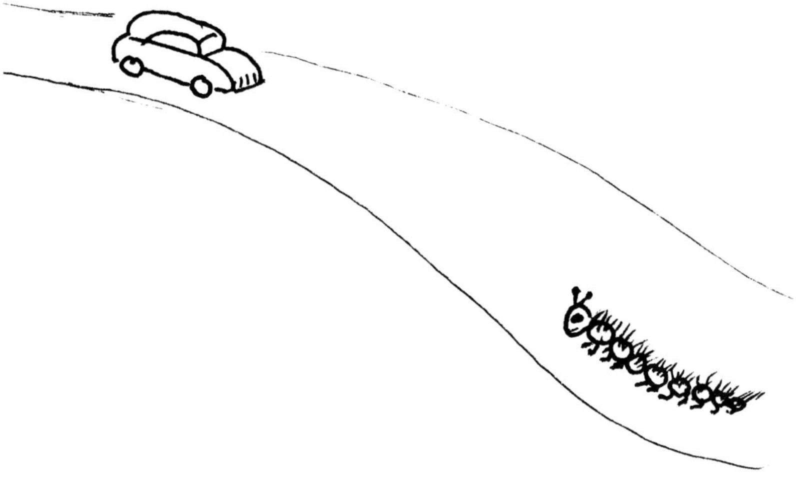

WOOD ANTS

I'm sitting in the oak wood
There's movement all around
Everything is moving
Especially the ground.

I take a closer look
There are wood ants everywhere
Long and brown and busy
Running here and there.

One crawls inside my welly boot
One bites me on the knee
I think I'll leave them to it
It's straight back home for me.

SLUGS

Slippery, slimy, slithery,
Sliding, slinking, slick,
Sleek, slow, sluggish
Slug.

MY DADDY DOESN'T LIKE SLUGS

My daddy doesn't like slugs,
He calls them dreadful names.
When something spoils his garden plants
They always get the blame.
He puts down little pellets,
Which they're supposed to eat,
He seems to think that this will do the trick,
But little does he realise
That I go and pick them up.
I don't want to see those big slugs being sick.

APHID

Aphid
Small
Green
Transparent wing
Aphid
Watch out
Ladybird about!

COCOON

Caterpillar's gone
Not dead
Not sleeping
But transforming
To reappear one day
In a different form
As a butterfly
So leave him for now
In his changing room.

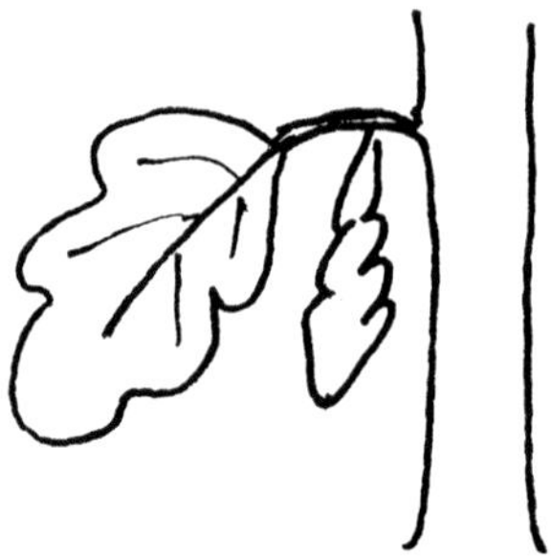

EARWIG

My granny has just told me
That there's something on my ear.
She took a look and said it was an earwig.
I flicked it off in horror
But it never reached the floor –
It landed in the middle of her wig!

PICNIC TIME

It's a lovely warm day
And mum says as a treat
We can take our lunch outside
In the garden to eat.
We set up the table
Take out the seats
Choose a place in the shade
To keep out of the heat

It couldn't be nicer
Well, that's what we thought
Then along came the wasps
In a full scale assault
We try to ignore them
'cause that's what we're taught
But then the screams start
It's not really our fault.

They buzz round our ears
And crawl on our forks
Try and get in my mouth
When I eat or talk

On my strawberry jelly
They go for a walk
There seem to be wasps
Wherever you look.

We flap at them
Shout at them
As they buzz around
My dinner goes flying
And falls to the ground
My sister is screaming
My mum can't be found.
I give up – I'm going.
The wasps won this round.

CRANEFLY

Legs so spindly
Legs so long
Legs so tickly
Not too strong
Hear them flying in the night
Buzzing as they hit the light.

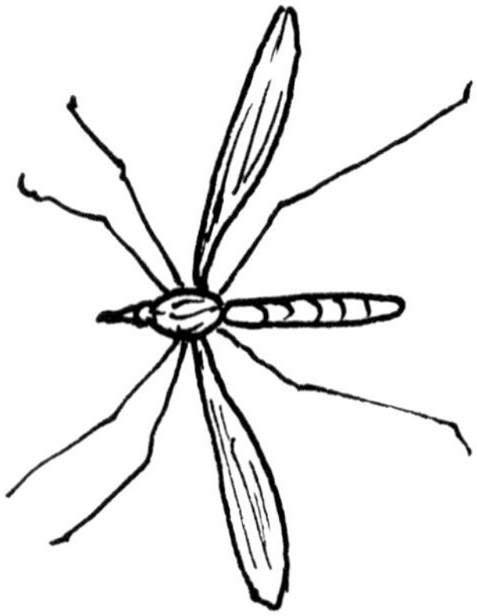

MOTHS

Put on a light
Late at night
Open the door
And in they'll pour,
Moths, moths,
Different shapes and sizes
Different patterns and disguises.

MOSQUITO BITES

I never saw it bite me
I didn't feel it sting
But now my leg is itching
And I cannot do a thing.

There's big white lumps right up my leg
And I'm not allowed to scratch it.
If I see that mosquito near me again
He's really going to catch it!

GRASSHOPPER

I can hear you in the garden
A high-pitched scratching sound
I look for you amongst the grass
How come you can't be found?

FLY BY NIGHT

I'm trying to get to sleep
Lying in my bed
When a fly appears from nowhere
And starts buzzing round my head

It circles the room like a fighter plane
Dive bombing my face
It sounds more like a rocket
Orbiting in space

I turn on the light to have a look
And of course the buzzing stops
But there it goes again
When I turn the light switch off

It's making such an awful noise
That I call it a rude name
I hide my head beneath the quilt
But I can hear it all the same

I try to just ignore it
And get to sleep instead
But in the end I give up
And leave my cosy bed

I find a book to whack it with
Although I know it's cruel
But I couldn't see or hear it
I really feel a fool.

All is quiet, I get to bed
There's nothing to be done
Though I know he'll wake me up again
Before the morning comes

BEES

Busy, buzzing bees
Go somewhere else, please
And let me finish off my little doze.
Busy, buzzing bees
Just leave me in peace
Buzz off and go and find another rose.

SPIDER, SPIDER

Spider, Spider on the wall
Why is it you never fall?
Spider, Spider in mid-air
What is it that holds you there?
Spider, Spider above my head
Please don't creep into my bed.

PANIC

I could see out the corner of my eye
Something move across the floor
A spider the size of a dinner plate
Was moving towards the door.

H … h … help! I cried. I leapt up
And jumped on to the table
I shouted, yelled, screeched and screamed
As loud as I was able.

Mum came in, she took one look
And sprang on to a chair.
All afternoon that's where we'll be
Until my dad comes home for tea!

SPIDER'S WEB

A spider's web is a beautiful sight
Especially in the morning
When the dewdrops catch the light

Delicately made with precision and care
Spun with fine thread
And suspended in the air

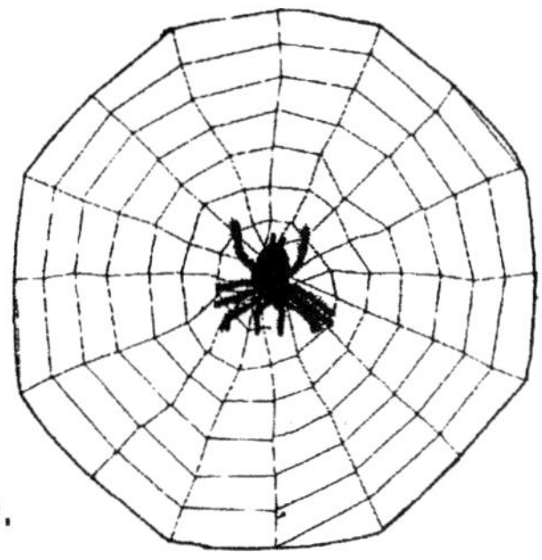

A dangerous trap
To the insects that fly
Deadly and cruel –
If you get caught, you die.

A spider's web is a necessary thing
Especially if you're the spider
For there isn't a creature can survive
Without a bit of food inside her.

SPIDER IN THE BATH

What are you doing in my bath?
Good job that I saw you first.
Mother would have had a fit
She screams and jumps as if she'll burst.

Come on out you little beast
Before I put the water on
Mum will be up in a minute
You've got no choice, you must be gone.

Up the side – you're almost there
Bother, down you fall again
Hurry up, I know it's slippery
You mustn't end up down the drain.

Oh no, too late. I'm sure she's coming.
I'll put my hands over my ears
It starts with yelling then with screaming
And it always ends in tears.

That's funny, mother's in the bathroom
But there hasn't been a sound.
You little sneak, where are you hiding?
On the ceiling? On the ground?

She's running the water, just hope you're out.
Oh well, I expect I'll see you about.

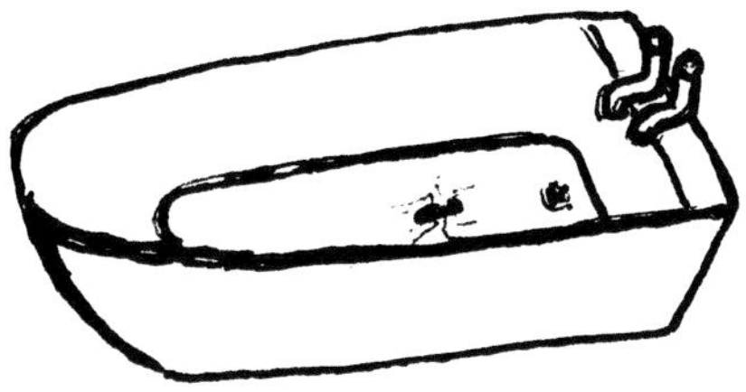

ARE YOU A PEST?

Snails

Slowly, slowly
On we go
Moving quietly
Always slow
Home on back
We are the snails.
Where are we going?
Follow our trails
Over the wall
Under the pot.
Are you a pest?
Certainly not!

(But I think you are!)

Ladybirds

Pretty little ladybird,
Pretty little ladybird
A speck of scarlet in the sky
You can't miss me flying by
Red coat and black spot.
Are you a pest?
Certainly not!

Spiders

Running here, running there
Spinning webs, everywhere
In dark corners
Lurking there
Darting out
Give you a scare
After you, like a shot.
Are you a pest?
Certainly not!

Bees

Bzz, bzzz, busy bee
Bzz, bzzz, busy bee
Bzz, bzzz, making honey
Bzz, bzzz, velvety
Bzz, bzzz, a sting we've got
Are you a pest?
Certainly not!

Butterflies

Graceful and pretty
We fly through the air
Up and down
And here and there
We find a flower to settle on
Bask in the sun
But not for long
Silent and beautiful
Wings we have got
Are you a pest?
Certainly not!

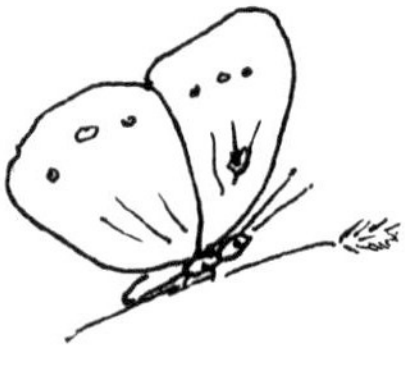

Centipedes

Tickly, wriggly
Off we go
How many legs?
We don't know
Tickly, wiggly centipede
On living roots and plants we feed.
So you're the pest, not all the rest.
Are you a pest?
I suppose so – yes!